RV Cooking

Best
Road Trip Recipes
for RV Living and
Campsite Cooking

Louise Davidson

ISBN: 978-1720386254

Printed in the United States

Contents

Introduction

This compilation of recipes was created with some special people in mind. A lot of them, actually, and I've listed some of them here:

- People who need help in planning their meals for their next RV vacation.
- People who don't think that going camping or RVing means cooking tasteless food made from highly-processed ingredients.
- People who just want to get away and still be able to prepare not-so-elaborate but oh-so-tasty meals.
- People who've never tried RVing and are a bit overwhelmed by the thought of having to cook in a small kitchen with limited equipment.
- People who know how much they can save by using what they have in their RV for preparing meals while on a trip.
- RVers who've already tried amazing dishes on their trips and are still looking for more.
- People who believe that the cooking should be just as much of an adventure as the trip.
- People who like food with funny names like Hobo Pie, Poor Man's Lobster, and Dump Cake.
- People who want to balance being close to nature with not being too far from the convenience of their kitchen.
- First timers and veteran RVers alike. Even if you've been RVing for years, there are recipes here that will still surprise you.
- People who want to convince the world that RVing doesn't mean leaving behind good food and good cooking.
- People who want to relax and enjoy the trip but still eat delicious, healthy, and satisfying food.

- People who want to get away and get close to nature but aren't willing to give up yummy desserts to do it.
- People who want to prepare simple but delicious food on their trip and not have to do a lot of cleaning up afterwards.
- Owners of a Dutch oven who know there are an endless number of dishes that can be prepared using it.
- People who like the idea of cooking a snack, dinner, pasta, soup or even dessert, by the campfire.
- People who want to come back to their RV after a long day of activities and exploration looking forward to a freshly-cooked, hearty meal.
- Adults and children alike who see preparing food outdoors or over a campfire as fun.

As you see, there certainly are many different kinds of people who will appreciate the recipes here. I've tried putting together recipes that aren't too complicated, and I've striven for variety so that absolutely everyone can find something to love and enjoy.

Cooking Equipment & Utensils

Aside from basic essentials like a few pots and pans, a large wooden spoon, a chef's knife and cutting board, and knives, forks, spoons, cups, bowls and plates for serving, there are some particularly useful items for an RV trip that are worth mentioning here.

Aluminum foil – You may not even need to bring any other cookware, because you can cook a meal, a snack and even dessert by wrapping ingredients in foil and cooking over the campfire, a grill, or hot coals. Foil is also a life saver when you're wary of cooking on the rusty-looking grill at the campsite or other questionable surfaces. Double your layers to avoid tearing, or use heavy-duty foil.

Briquettes – Compressed charcoal and other materials which are lit and allowed to heat up for cooking with a grill or Dutch oven. There are self-lighting briquettes that already contain lighter fluid and are easy to light, but they give off an unpleasant odor. Regular charcoal briquettes may take a little more time to get going, but they help lend a smoky flavor to food.

Cast iron skillet – Its versatility allows you to use it for dishes from breakfast hash to steaks to cakes. Cast iron distributes heat well and so is ideal for cooking over charcoal or firewood. A well-seasoned skillet can be just as good, if not better, than a nonstick pan.

Charcoal or Gas Grill – Parks and campsites usually provide grills, but you may not be comfortable using their rusty-looking grates. Veteran campers recommend lining suspicious-looking grates with aluminum foil to be safe, but you could just bring your own portable grill.

Dutch oven – the Dutch oven just might be your best friend during your trip. It can easily serve as a makeshift oven for preparing favorites like pot roasts, stews, pasta dishes, breads, and cakes.

Campers usually use an outdoor Dutch oven with legs which make it ideal for cooking over coals. The shape of the lid allows you to place coals on top, too. Usually, the Dutch oven is placed on top of a ring of coals or briquettes. The rule is "diameter in inches minus three" for the bottom and "diameter in inches plus three," for the top. In other words, if your Dutch oven has a 10-inch diameter, you would use a ring of 7 briquettes underneath and 13 briquettes on top.

Hobo Pie Maker – An ingenious contraption that makes it easy and fun to prepare sandwiches and even desserts on the campfire.

Meat thermometer – Even the most experienced cooks can have a hard time knowing when a meat dish is done. A thermometer will make it easier for you to determine when the meat is ready – and eliminate the risk of your trip being ruined by food poisoning from improperly-cooked meat.

Nonstick cooking spray – Not only is it convenient to use, but it can also mean a few less calories in the dish.

Ziploc bags – Convenient and space saving. You can use them for storing precooked pasta, marinades, herbs, spices, cut-up veggies, and almost anything you can think of. This will help simplify and organize your cooking.

RV Cooking Tips

- RV or camping food doesn't have to be tasteless and unimaginative. Bring some spices along, and take advantage of fresh herbs and other produce you'll find along the way.
- Try to limit the number of cooking pots and utensils you use to prepare your meals. Simplify. Cooking in foil, for example, does away with having to wash heavy cookware after meal preparation
- Using pre-grated cheese is not normally recommended as such cheese has been slightly modified to keep the shreds separate, which affects the taste and consistency when cooked. But this time, we're after the extra convenience, so it wouldn't hurt to compromise while on the road.
- Always open foil packets away from your face to avoid being blasted with hot steam.
- Plan your menu in advance and chop, slice or cut veggies and other ingredients at home. Add labels so you won't be guessing which recipe they're for.
- Condiments and sauces are easier to dispense using ketchup dispensers. They're useful when making pizza or sandwiches, for example.
- Dehydrated ingredients like vegetables and meat weigh less and do not require refrigeration; neither do they spoil easily.
- Save the fat and bacon drippings – they're great adding flavor to cast iron skillet recipes
- Store dry herbs and spices in old Tic Tac® boxes.
- Precooking bacon or sausages at home saves a lot of time and mess on the road.
- Before leaving home, clean empty condiment bottles and fill them with pancake batter, cake batter, or premixed

omelets to take along with you for an easy meal. Same can be said for dry preparation for pancakes, cakes, trail mixes, spice blends like Italian spices, and barbecue rubs, just to name a few.

Not all RVs are created equal, so I have not included recipes that require equipment like a standard oven, blender, or microwave. While preparing and compiling these recipes, I had only the most basic RV kitchen - or "galley", in RV lingo. Most of the recipes have been created to favor more outdoor-type cooking. I'm sure you'll enjoy them. Although you may find some a bit challenging, most of them are simple and all of them are delicious and fun!

Food Safety and
Other Things to Consider

I would not feel comfortable without any words on food safety and this is especially true when you are on the road or at the campsite.

When cooking outdoors, it is important to be diligent when it comes to food safety. Whether you have a portable refrigerator in your camper or you are depending upon your trusty cooler and ice or ice packs, keeping perishable foods at a temperature of 40°F or lower is priority number one. It takes barely any time at all for food-borne bacteria to invade your perishables. It is a good idea to bring along at least one if not several food thermometers to monitor the temperature of foods both during refrigeration and during cooking. Also, never leave cooked food sitting out too long. Once you are finished eating, any leftovers should be properly packaged and refrigerated.

Take care in double securing any raw meat or prepared meals that contain raw meats. Do not store any ingredients that may be eaten raw in the same container that you use to store your uncooked meat products. The unplanned leaking of meat juices can potentially contaminate produce and other food items, turning a fun camping trip into a very unpleasant one.

Use a meat thermometer to check the internal temperature of meats before consuming. All poultry and ground meat mixtures should be cooked to an internal temperature of 165°F. Beef has a bit of wider range of acceptable temperatures based on doneness preference. Beef should be cooked to at least 145°F (acceptable safe rare to medium-rare temperature) up to 170°F (well done all of the way through). These guidelines also need to be followed for any ingredients that have had contact with raw meat within the packets.

For your convenience, we added at the end of the book, in the appendix, useful charts and tables for cooking. It includes a cooking conversion charts, internal temperature cooking charts for meats, poultry, and fish, barbecue grilling times, a brief guide for cooking with cast iron Dutch oven, and a foil packets how to section. It starts on page 77.

We are now ready to start cooking!

Breakfast, Snacks, and Sandwiches

Spiced Scones

Serves: 6
Preparation Time: 15 minutes
Cooking Time: 10 minutes

Ingredients
2 cups self-rising flour
1 teaspoon cumin
⅛ teaspoon red pepper flakes, or to taste
¼ teaspoon salt
2 tablespoons butter
¾ cup milk

Directions
1. In a bowl, combine flour, cumin, chili and salt.
2. Rub in butter until coarse-textured.
3. Add milk and mix.
4. Press out on a floured surface to make a ¾-inch thick round.
5. Cut into 6 wedges.
6. Cook in a nonstick frying pan or well-seasoned skillet over medium heat until browned and cooked through (about 5 minutes on each side).

Nutrition (per serving)
Calories 186
Carbs 31.4 g
Fat 4.8 g
Protein 1.7 g
Sodium 670 mg

Breakfast Scramble

Serves: 2
Preparation Time: 5 minutes
Cooking Time: 15 minutes

Ingredients
4 small red potatoes, diced
¼ cup water
1 tablespoon olive oil
Pinch of salt
4 large eggs, beaten
1 tablespoon milk
1 scallion, thinly sliced
⅓ cup grated cheese
1 tablespoon freshly thyme or herb of choice, chopped

Directions
1. Combine potatoes, water, oil and salt in a nonstick frying pan or well-seasoned skillet.
2. Cover and cook over high heat until almost all the water has dried out and potatoes begin to sizzle in the oil (about 5 minutes).
3. Remove lid and flip potatoes, cooking until lightly browned (about 5 minutes).
4. Beat the eggs and milk in a bowl.
5. Pour over the potatoes.
6. Add sliced scallion and mix to scramble until set (about 3 minutes).
7. Remove from heat.
8. Sprinkle with cheese and herbs.
9. Let sit until cheese melts (about 1 minute) and serve.

Nutrition (per serving)
Calories 342
Carbs 15.5 g
Fat 22.7 g
Protein 19.3 g
Sodium 425 mg

Breakfast Cinnamon Rolls

Serves: 6
Preparation Time: 10 minutes
Cooking Time: 20–30 minutes

Ingredients

2 (7½-ounce) packages buttermilk biscuits
¼ cup butter, melted or softened to spreadable consistency
¾ cup brown sugar, packed
1 teaspoon cinnamon
½ cup nuts or raisins (optional)

Frosting
1½ cups powdered sugar
¼ cup butter softened
1 teaspoon vanilla extract
2 tablespoons milk or a little more, to get right consistency

Directions

1. Heat up coals until very hot. For a 2- to 2¾- quart Dutch oven (about 8-inch diameter), set aside 5 coals for the bottom and 11 for the top.
2. Spray with nonstick spray or rub the inside with a little oil.
3. Remove the biscuits from the packages and roll out thinly.
4. Spread evenly with melted butter.
5. Sprinkle as evenly as possible with sugar, cinnamon, and nuts or raisins (if using).
6. Roll into rods. Note: These may be made in advance, wrapped in plastic and frozen; allow them to thaw out during the trip.
7. Arrange in Dutch oven, cutting as needed to make them fit.
8. Position over coals and place lid with coals on top.

9. Check about 18 minutes into cooking. Adjust the heat by removing or adding coals, as needed. Rotate the Dutch oven to ensure even heating.
10. Roll should be done in 20–30 minutes. It should be fragrant and no longer doughy.
11. Remove from heat and let cool while you prepare the frosting (about 5 minutes).
12. Combine the sugar, butter and vanilla. Gradually add the milk until the desired consistency is attained. It should be thick and pourable but not watery.
13. Drizzle over cooked roll, or cut into pieces and drizzle with frosting individually.

Nutrition (per serving)
Calories 656
Carbs 112.7 g
Fat 25.8 g
Protein 5.7 g
Sodium 994 mg

Eggs with Beans and Tomatoes

Serves: 2
Preparation Time: 5 minutes
Cooking Time: 12–15 minutes

Ingredients
2 tablespoons olive or canola oil
1 medium red onion, minced
2 teaspoons cumin
½ teaspoon red pepper flakes, or to taste
Salt and pepper, to taste
1 (14-ounce) can chopped or diced tomatoes
½ (15-ounce) can cannellini beans
4 eggs
Fresh herbs of choice (like rosemary, basil or sage), chopped

Directions
1. Heat oil in a nonstick pan or cast iron skillet over medium heat.
2. Add onion and spices and sauté until fragrant (about 1 minute).
3. Season with salt and pepper.
4. Add tomatoes and beans.
5. Continue cooking, with occasional stirring, until onion is tender (about 5 minutes).
6. Make 4 depressions in mixture and crack an egg into each.
7. Cover and let cook until eggs are desired doneness (about 2–5 minutes).
8. Season again, as needed, and sprinkle with herbs.
9. Serve while hot.

Nutrition (per serving)
Calories 354
Carbs 21.1 g
Fat 23.2 g
Protein 17.9 g
Sodium 1028 mg

Grilled Roast Beef Paninis

Serves: 1–2
Preparation Time: 5 minutes
Cooking Time: 2 minutes

Ingredients
2 slices Italian bread (like ciabatta or michetta)
1 tablespoon aioli garlic mustard
2 slices roast beef
2 slices provolone cheese
½ green pepper, grilled (optional)
2 tablespoons butter

Directions
1. Spread aioli over one side of each bread slice.
2. Place roast beef, cheese and green pepper (if using) over one slice.
3. Place remaining bread slice on top.
4. Butter the outside of the bread slices.
5. Wrap in foil and place on grill or in hobo pie maker.
6. Grill until done (about 1–3 minutes, depending on heat from campfire).

Nutrition (per serving)
Calories 349
Carbs 10.1 g
Fat 24 g
Protein 23.7 g
Sodium 745 mg

Basic Hobo Pie

Serves: 5–6
Preparation Time: 5 minutes
Cooking Time: 1–3 minutes

Ingredients
1 loaf bread, sliced thickly into squares
¼ cup pizza sauce
Mozzarella cheese, sliced thinly or shredded
10–15 slices pepperoni, chopped
¼ cup butter, softened, or nonstick cooking spray

Directions
1. To prevent sticking, butter the bread slices that will be the outer sides or the sandwiches; or simply spray the inside of the hobo pie maker with nonstick cooking spray.
2. Lay a slice, buttered side down (if not using nonstick spray) on the hobo pie maker.
3. Layer with pizza sauce (be sparing, as too much will spill out and burn), cheese and pepperoni.
4. Top with second slice of bread, buttered side up (if using butter).
5. Wrap in aluminum foil, if desired, for easier clean up.
6. Close pie maker and place over coals, turning now and then until bread is toasted (about 1–3 minutes; heat from campfires varies a lot).

Other suggested Hobo Pie variations:
- chocolate and marshmallows (s'mores)
- blueberry pie filling and butter or cream cheese
- ham and cheese
- peach pie filling and marshmallow
- peanut butter, marshmallow and chocolate (rocky road)

- Nutella and strawberries
- sausage, egg and cheese
- tuna and cheese
- use biscuit dough instead of bread

Nutrition (per serving)
Calories 220
Carbs 25.7 g
Fat 8.8 g
Protein 9.1 g
Sodium 558 mg

Backcountry Breakfast

Serves: 2
Preparation Time: 5–10 minutes
Cooking Time: 0 minutes

Ingredients
¾ cup quick-cooking or instant oats
¼ cup powdered milk
⅓ cup raisins or dried apple bits
⅓ cup unsalted mixed nuts, chopped
2 teaspoons unsalted shelled sunflower seeds (optional)
1½ tablespoons brown sugar
½ teaspoon cinnamon
2 cups boiling water

Directions
1. Prepare in advance: Combine ingredients except boiling water in a Ziploc bag, shaking to mix. Set aside until ready for use.
2. To serve, place mixture in a bowl and add boiling water. Let sit for 2 minutes. Mix and serve.

Nutrition (per serving)
Calories 343
Carbs 54.2 g
Fat 14.4 g
Protein 8.5 g
Sodium 93 mg

Simple Pizza Turnovers

Serves: 8
Preparation Time: 5 minutes
Cooking Time: 15 minutes

Ingredients
8–16 slices pepperoni, diced
¼ cup shredded mozzarella cheese
3–4 tablespoons pizza or tomato sauce, or as needed
1 tube flaky biscuit dough (to make 8 biscuits)
2 tablespoons butter (optional)

Directions
1. In a bowl, mix pepperoni and mozzarella together.
2. Add pizza sauce gradually until pepperoni and cheese begin stick together.
3. Flatten a biscuit and place a small amount in the middle. Do the same for the rest of the biscuits, distributing the filling as equally as possible.
4. Fold over and press edges together to seal.
5. Arrange on a nonstick pan or skillet and place over medium heat.
6. Melt butter in pan and swirl to spread, if using.
7. When bottom is lightly browned, flip over to brown other side (about 10–12 minutes total).

Nutrition (per serving)
Calories 221
Carbs 25.1 g
Fat 11 g
Protein 5.6 g
Sodium 774 mg

Dutch Oven Pizza

Serves: 12 (yield: 2 pizzas)
Preparation Time: 20 minutes
Cooking Time: 15 minutes

Ingredients
Canola oil, for greasing, or nonstick cooking spray
1 tube pre-made pizza crust, divided
1 cup tomato or pizza sauce, divided
3 cups mozzarella cheese, shredded, divided
½ cup cheddar cheese, grated, divided
Dash of garlic powder
Salt and pepper, to taste
1 medium onion, sliced, divided
12 ounces pepperoni slices, divided

Directions
1. Heat up coals in a fire pit, shifting them to heat evenly.
2. Grease a Dutch oven.
3. Roll out tube of dough and divide into 2.
4. Spread one piece over bottom of Dutch oven, pressing and patching if needed. Note: If you want two pizzas but only have one Dutch oven, line with aluminum foil or an aluminum pie pan so that you can easily remove the first when cooked and then add the second one.
5. Spread half of sauce over dough.
6. Season with garlic powder, salt, and pepper.
7. Arrange half of pepperoni and half of onion on top.
8. Place over hot coals.
9. Place lid and add about 8 coals on top.

10. Cook until crust is lightly browned and no longer doughy (about 10 minutes). Meanwhile, prepare second pizza on a sheet of foil or in an aluminum foil pie pan using remaining ingredients (remember to leave out the cheese for now).
11. Sprinkle the first pizza with the cheese and replace the lid. Add a few more pieces of coal to melt cheese faster.
12. Remove from coals, let cool slightly, and remove pizza from Dutch oven.
13. Carefully place second pizza into Dutch oven and bake as above.

Nutrition (per serving)
Calories 329
Carbs 20.3 g
Fat 21.9 g
Protein 17.3 g
Sodium 1106 mg

Soups and Stews

Easiest Beef Stew

Serves: 4
Preparation Time: 2 minutes
Cooking Time: 10 minutes

Ingredients
1 pound lean ground beef
1 (15-ounce) can mixed vegetables
2 (11½-ounce) cans V–8 vegetable juice or tomato juice

Directions
1. Cook the ground beef in a Dutch oven in its own juices until evenly browned (about 8–10 minutes).
2. Drain off any juices.
3. Add the rest of the ingredients.
4. Bring to a boil.
5. Reduce heat and let simmer until all the vegetables are heated through.

Nutrition (per serving)
Calories 386
Carbs 16.8 g
Fat 23.7 g
Protein 23.8 g
Sodium 537 mg

Camper's Onion Soup in Foil

Serves: 1
Preparation Time: 5 minutes
Cooking Time: 40–60 minutes

Ingredients
1 large onion
1 beef bouillon cube, crumbled
1–2 tablespoons softened or melted butter
Dash of black pepper (optional)
Grated Parmesan and/or Swiss cheese, for sprinkling
1 slice baguette or any bread of choice, toasted

Directions
1. Butter one side of a thick sheet of aluminum (large enough to cover the whole onion, plus extra for twisting to seal and to serve as a 'tail' for easy handling).
2. Peel the onion and core like an apple, but not all the way to the bottom; leave a 'well' at the center.
3. Fill the well with crumbled bouillon and butter.
4. Fold the aluminum over the onion and twist the ends to seal.
5. Place in coals, over grill or around edges of campfire (find a place where heat is moderate and relatively even).
6. Cook until tender or easy to squeeze with tongs (about 40–60 minutes).
7. Place in a bowl and open the foil.
8. Sprinkle with black pepper and cheese.
9. Serve with a baguette slice.

Nutrition (per serving)
Calories 299
Carbs 25.9 g
Fat 19.6 g
Protein 6.1 g
Sodium 1152 mg

Corn and Sweet Potato Chowder

Serves: 4
Preparation Time: 10 minutes
Cooking Time: 20 minutes

Ingredients
4 bacon strips, chopped
1 medium onion, diced
2 (11-ounce) cans whole kernel corn, liquid drained into a separate container
2 cups water
1 (14.75-ounce) can cream of corn
4 medium-sized sweet potatoes, peeled and diced
Salt and pepper, to taste

Directions
1. Cook the bacon in a deep pot until crisp. Optional: Scoop or drain out rendered fat as desired, leaving just enough to sauté onion.
2. Add onion and sauté until transparent (about 3–5 minutes).
3. Pour in water and corn liquid.
4. Bring to a boil.
5. Add sweet potatoes and cook until tender (about 5 minutes).
6. Stir in kernels and cream of corn.
7. Cook until heated through.
8. Season with salt and pepper.

Nutrition (per serving)
Calories 158
Carbs 24.2 g
Fat 3.3 g
Protein 8.5 g
Sodium 919 mg

Poultry

Campers' Chicken Chili

Serves: 2
Preparation Time: 5 minutes
Cooking Time: 15–20 minutes

Ingredients
1 tablespoon cooking oil
1 medium onion, diced
1 medium carrot, peeled and sliced
1 medium celery stalk, sliced
1 cup chicken stock
1 (about 6-ounce) chicken breast, boneless, skinless, cut into bite-size pieces
½ (15-ounce) can cannellini beans, drained and rinsed
1 teaspoon ground cumin
Chili flakes, to taste
Salt and pepper, to taste

Directions
1. Heat oil in a skillet or saucepan over medium heat.
2. Sauté onion, carrot, and celery until fragrant and slightly darkened in color (about 2 minutes).
3. Stir in spices with chicken. Cook until fragrant and chicken becomes white on the surface (about 3 minutes).
4. Pour in stock and bring to a simmer. Cook until vegetables are tender and chicken is cooked through (about 7–10 minutes).
5. Add beans and heat to cook through (about 2 minutes).
6. Adjust flavor with salt and pepper, as needed.
7. Serve hot.

Nutrition (per serving)
Calories 327
Carbs 29.1 g
Fat 11.6 g
Protein 29 g
Sodium 767 mg

Grilled Barbecue Chicken

Serves: 4
Preparation Time: 10 minutes
Cooking Time: 25 minutes

Ingredients
4 (4-ounce) boneless, skinless chicken breasts
Salt and pepper, to taste
½ cup barbecue sauce of choice, or to taste
1 medium zucchini, sliced thinly
1 bell pepper, cut into thin strips
4 asparagus spears
2 tablespoons extra virgin olive oil, for drizzling

Directions
1. Stack 2 sheets of aluminum foil, big enough to wrap one chicken breast, to make 1 foil packet.
2. Place 1 chicken breast at the center and season with salt and pepper.
3. Drizzle with 1 tablespoon (or more, if desired) of barbecue sauce.
4. Surround the chicken breast with a fourth each of the zucchini and bell pepper.
5. Add 1 asparagus spear and drizzle everything with about 1 teaspoon of extra-virgin olive oil.
6. Fold the sides of the foil over the chicken and seal.
7. Repeat with the remaining ingredients (to make 4 foil packets).
8. Grill until chicken is cooked through and veggies are tender (about 20–25 minutes, turning over midway through cooking).
9. Let rest for about 3–5 minutes before serving.

Nutrition (per serving)
Calories 364
Carbs 22 g
Fat 3 g
Protein 25 g
Sodium 510 mg

Turkey Chili

Serves: 6
Preparation Time: 5 minutes
Cooking Time: 90–120 minutes

Ingredients
2 tablespoons olive oil
1 large onion, diced
3 garlic cloves
2 pounds ground turkey
1 (28-ounce) can plum tomatoes
1 (24-ounce) can or jar tomato sauce
1 (18-ounce) can kidney beans
½ can black beans
3 tablespoons hot chili sauce, or to taste
1 teaspoon paprika
2 teaspoons cumin
2 teaspoons chili powder, or to taste
1 teaspoon cayenne, or to taste
Salt, to taste

Directions
1. In a heavy-bottomed saucepan or pot, heat oil over medium heat.
2. Add onion and garlic. Sauté until fragrant (about 1 minute).
3. Add ground turkey and cook, stirring occasionally, until well- and evenly browned.
4. Stir in plum tomatoes, tomato sauce, and beans.
5. Add spices and continue stirring to blend.
6. Bring to a simmer, cover, and cook for 1½ to 2 hours.

Nutrition (per serving)
Calories 389
Carbs 31.4 g
Fat 13.1 g
Protein 39.1 g
Sodium 1593 mg

Grilled Turkey Breast

Serves: 4
Preparation Time: 5 minutes plus 2 hours refrigeration
Cooking Time: 40 minutes

Ingredients
1 (3–4-pound) turkey breast, bone-in
Salt and pepper, to taste
2 tablespoons vegetable oil

Brine
¼ cup salt
¼ cup sugar
2 cups water

Directions
1. Combine brine ingredients in a large Ziploc bag. Shake to dissolve granules.
2. Place turkey breast in brine and keep chilled (at 40°F) for 2 hours.
3. Preheat grill.
4. After brining, remove turkey breast, rinse, and pat dry.
5. Season with salt and pepper. (Note: Brining does not necessarily make the meat taste salty, especially if done for a short duration.)
6. Sear the skin side of the turkey breast over high heat.
7. Turn off one side of grill or, if using charcoal, move charcoal to the sides and place breast, skin side up, on grate over cleared space.
8. Cook over residual heat until browned and juices run clear (about 30–40 minutes or longer, depending on size), flipping over once or twice if needed. If you have a meat thermometer, internal temperature of thickest part should be about 160°F.
9. Remove from heat and cover or tent with foil. Let sit for about 15 minutes before serving.

Nutrition (per serving)
Calories 644
Carbs 0 g
Fat 25.2 g
Protein 97.8 g
Sodium 361 mg

Chicken Kebabs

Serves: 4
Preparation Time: 15 minutes plus 2–4 hours marinating time
Cooking Time: 10 minutes

Ingredients
2 to 2½ pounds chicken breast or thigh, skinless, boneless, cut into 1½-inch chunks
2 medium onions, quartered, layers separated
4 tomatoes, quartered

Marinade
⅓ cup butter
⅓ cup olive oil
½ cup fresh lemon juice
1 tablespoon oregano
Salt and pepper, to taste

Directions
1. Melt the butter in a saucepan and remove from heat.
2. Stir in the rest of the marinade ingredients.
3. Mix well.
4. Set aside about 2 tablespoons for basting and then pour the rest over chicken cubes.
5. Cover and let marinate for 2–4 hours.
6. If using wooden skewers, soak in warm water for 30 minutes before using (you'll need about 4–6 pieces).
7. Skewer ingredients alternately, starting with chicken, followed by onion, and then by tomato.
8. Cook on a grill over hot coals, basting and turning, until chicken is cooked through and veggies are slightly charred at the edges (about 10 minutes).

Nutrition (per serving)
Calories 434
Carbs 10.3 g
Fat 27.1 g
Protein 39 g
Sodium 1850 mg

Jerk Chicken

Serves: 2
Preparation Time: 10 minutes plus 30 minutes marinating time
Cooking Time: 20 minutes

Ingredients
2 large chicken breasts (about 16 ounces), skinless, boneless
Nonstick cooking spray

Jerk Sauce
2 small fresh jalapeno peppers, seeded
4 cloves garlic, peeled
2 tablespoons chicken broth
1 tablespoon plus 1 teaspoon vegetable oil
2 teaspoons paprika
1½ teaspoons dried thyme
1 teaspoon allspice
½ teaspoon salt
¼ teaspoon ground red pepper

Directions
1. Wipe the chicken dry with paper towels and make slashes on the surface.
2. Combine the ingredients for the jerk sauce in a blender. Blend well.
3. Coat the chicken with about half the jerk sauce and let marinate for about 30 minutes.
4. Spray and preheat grill.
5. Place chicken on grill.
6. Cook the chicken while brushing with more sauce and flipping frequently until chicken is no longer pink inside (about 20 minutes).
7. Goes well with rice, beans, and/or a salad.

Nutrition (per serving)
Calories 334
Carbs 3.4 g
Fat 11 g
Protein 54.3 g
Sodium 644 mg

Buttermilk Fried Chicken

Serves: 3–4
Preparation Time: 20 minutes plus 1 hour soaking time
Cooking Time: 50–60 minutes

Ingredients
1 (2½-pound) fryer chicken, cut up
1 cup buttermilk
Cooking oil, for frying

Coating
1 cup all-purpose flour
1½ teaspoons salt
½ teaspoon pepper

Gravy
¼ cup drippings from fried chicken
3 tablespoons all-purpose flour
1 cup milk
1½ cups water, or as needed
Salt and pepper, to taste

Directions
1. Wipe chicken dry with paper towels and then soak in the buttermilk, refrigerated, for 1 hour. Drain well after soaking.
2. Prepare mixture for coating by combining ingredients in a bowl or double-strength paper bag.
3. Dredge the chicken with the flour mixture. Coat well and shake off any excess.
4. Let sit for 15 minutes.
5. Heat up about ½ to 1 inch of oil in a skillet.
6. Add chicken to heated oil. (Do not crowd; if skillet is small, do this in batches.)

7. Fry, flipping over from time to time, until browned on the surface but not done inside (about 6 minutes).
8. Reduce heat, cover and let simmer for about 30–40 minutes, flipping occasionally, until juices run clear.
9. Remove cover, increasing heat as needed, and let cook 5 minutes longer or until surface is golden brown and crisp.
10. Remove from skillet and drain over paper towels.
11. Carefully drain out drippings in skillet, leaving about ¼ cup.
12. Stir in flour and cook until bubbly.
13. Stir in milk and water.
14. Cook, with stirring, until thickened.
15. Add a little more water, if needed, to adjust consistency.
16. Season with salt and pepper.
17. Serve chicken with the gravy on the side.

Nutrition (per serving)
Calories 660
Carbs 28.6 g
Fat 14.1 g
Protein 97.4 g
Sodium 1428 mg

Smothered Chicken

Serves: 2
Preparation Time: 10 minutes
Cooking Time: 15–20 minutes

Ingredients
2 chicken breasts, skinless
Garlic salt, to taste
Salt-free herb seasoning of choice, to taste
½ small green bell pepper, sliced
½ small onion, sliced
⅓ cup mozzarella cheese, or to taste

Directions
1. Season chicken with garlic salt and herb seasoning.
2. Wrap in 2 stacked sheets of aluminum foil.
3. Place on grill.
4. After about 6 minutes, flip over.
5. Cook about 2 minutes longer.
6. Carefully open foil and add bell pepper and onion.
7. Reseal foil and let cook until almost done (about 8 minutes, depending on size of chicken breast and heat of grill).
8. Open foil again and add cheese. Reseal.
9. Cook until cheese is melted and chicken is fully cooked (about 2 minutes).

Nutrition (per serving)
Calories 304
Carbs 2.7 g
Fat 5 g
Protein 59.2 g
Sodium 463 mg

Pork and Beef

Country Style Ribs

Serves: 6
Preparation Time: 10 minutes plus 24 hours marinating time
Cooking Time: 35 minutes

Ingredients
6 pounds country style pork ribs
Barbecue sauce, for basting

Marinade
3 tablespoons olive oil
⅓ cup hoisin sauce
⅓ cup soy sauce
4 teaspoons minced ginger
¾ cup whisky
Zest of one orange
Juice of one orange
½ cup light brown sugar
6 cloves garlic, minced
2 cups barbeque sauce

Directions
1. Place ribs in a large pot or Dutch oven and cover with water. Bring to a boil and continue until partly cooked (about 20 minutes). Drain well.
2. Combine ingredients for marinade.
3. Place ribs with marinade in a shallow container with lid or in a large Ziploc bag.
4. Let marinate, refrigerated, for 24 hours to 2 days.
5. Bring to room temperature before grilling.
6. Grill over medium heat for about 15 minutes, flipping frequently and basting with barbecue sauce.

Nutrition (per serving)
Calories 985
Carbs 23.5 g
Fat 56 g
Protein 94.1 g
Sodium 1025 mg

Walking Tacos

Serves: 2–4
Preparation Time: 10 minutes
Cooking Time: 10 minutes

Ingredients
1 pound ground beef
1 packet taco seasoning mix
1 medium tomato, chopped
¼ head lettuce, shredded
1 small onion, chopped
1 cup shredded cheese of choice (like cheddar or Monterey)
½ cup sour cream
¼ cup taco sauce
2–4 individual bags of corn chips, opened neatly on top

Directions
1. Brown beef over medium heat in a nonstick pan or cast-iron skillet.
2. Add seasoning and cook according to package instructions.
3. Divide into 2–4, depending on number of packets.
4. Add to packets of corn chips.
5. Add other ingredients as desired.
6. Stir with a fork and eat directly from the packets.

Nutrition (per serving)
Calories 653
Carbs 23.4 g
Fat 48.6 g
Protein 31 g
Sodium 558 mg

Camper's Beer Braised Short Ribs

Serves: 3–4
Preparation Time: 10 minutes
Cooking Time: Slow Cooker: 8 hours; Dutch Oven: 2 hours

Ingredients

3 pounds beef short ribs, bone-in
3 medium onions, cut into wedges
1 bay leaf

Sauce
1 (12-ounce) bottle beer
2 tablespoons brown sugar
2 tablespoons Dijon mustard
2 tablespoons tomato paste
2 teaspoons dried thyme
2 teaspoons beef bouillon granules
1 teaspoon salt
¼ teaspoon pepper

Slurry (optional)
3 tablespoons all-purpose flour
½ cup cold water

Directions

1. Slow Cooker: Place ribs, onions, and bay leaf in slow cooker. Combine sauce ingredients and add to ribs. Cover and cook for 8 hours on Low. Transfer ribs and onions to a bowl or wrap in foil and set aside. Heat the remaining juices in a saucepan over medium heat until reduced and thickened. If desired, mix slurry ingredients in a small bowl and stir into juices for a thicker sauce. Spoon over ribs and serve.

2. Dutch Oven: Arrange coals in a ring (about 7 briquettes) in the cooking pit, leaving a space at the center. Place ribs, onions, and bay leaf in Dutch oven. Mix sauce ingredients together and pour over ribs. Cover and place briquettes (about 13) in a ring on lid. Rotate lid every 30 minutes for even cooking and replace briquettes as needed. Cook until ribs can be pierced easily and flesh pulls away from the bone at the ends (internal temperature: 180–190°F). Transfer ribs and onions to a bowl or wrap in foil and set aside. Heat the remaining juices until reduced and thickened. If desired, mix slurry ingredients in a small bowl and stir into juices for a thicker sauce. Spoon over ribs and serve.

Nutrition (per serving)
Calories 418
Carbs 22 g
Fat 19 g
Protein 46 g
Sodium 821 mg

Tinfoil Sausage & Veggies

Serves: 4–6
Preparation Time: 15 minutes
Cooking Time: 10–20 minutes

Ingredients
1 red bell pepper, seeded and sliced thinly
2 ears shucked corn, cut into 1-inch disks
1 medium onion, chopped
4–5 small red potatoes cut into bite-size pieces
1 medium sized zucchini, sliced
1 (13-ounce) package smoked turkey sausage, sliced
Parsley, chopped, for sprinkling

Seasoning
5 tablespoons olive oil
1 tablespoon dried oregano
1 tablespoon dried parsley flakes
½ teaspoon garlic powder
1 teaspoon paprika
Salt and pepper, to taste

Directions
1. Mix seasoning ingredients together in a large bowl.
2. Add bell pepper, corn, onion, potatoes, zucchini, and sausage. Toss to coat with seasoning.
3. For one serving, stack two sheets of foil together or use one sheet of heavy-duty aluminum foil. Place about a fourth of the seasoned veggie-and-sausage mix at the center of the foil. Fold over and seal. Repeat with remaining ingredients.
4. Place on pre-heated grill and cook until veggies are crisp tender (about 10–20 minutes).
5. Remove from heat and serve sprinkled with chopped parsley.

Nutrition (per serving)
Calories 333
Carbs 31.2 g
Fat 17.1 g
Protein 16 g
Sodium 398 mg

Foil Hamburgers

Serves: 4
Preparation Time: 15 minutes
Cooking Time: 30–40 minutes

Ingredients
8 small new potatoes, unpeeled, quartered
1 teaspoon seasoned salt, or to taste
1 teaspoon Italian seasoning, or to taste
4 (¼-pound) frozen hamburger patties
1 cup frozen cut green beans
1 tablespoon olive oil

Directions
1. Stack 2 sheets of aluminum foil on top of each other (or use 1 sheet of heavy duty foil). Place 1 patty, ¼ of potatoes, and ¼ of green beans on the center of the stacked sheets. Sprinkle with about ¼ teaspoon each of seasoned salt, Italian seasoning (or to taste), and olive oil. Fold sides of foil over, leaving room for steam, and seal securely. Repeat for remaining ingredients.
2. Place on preheated grill at medium heat and cover. Let cook until patties are done (internal temperature: 160°F) and vegetables are tender (about 30–40 minutes), flipping the packets over midway through cooking.
3. Open carefully to release steam and serve.

Nutrition (per serving)
Calories 410
Carbs 41 g
Fat 16 g
Protein 25 g
Sodium 420 mg

Meal in a Can

Serves: 1
Preparation Time: 5 minutes
Cooking Time: 35–45 minutes

Ingredients
1 (about ¼-pound) hamburger patty
1 small red potato, quartered
⅓ medium carrot, peeled and cut into chunks
1 tablespoon chopped onion
½ small Roma tomato
2 tablespoons corn kernels
1 tablespoon butter or olive oil
Salt and pepper, to taste

Directions
1. Layer the ingredients as listed in a clean coffee can.
2. Cover tightly with foil. This may be kept in a cooler until the campfire or grill is ready.
3. Place on a grate over the campfire or coals, at about medium heat.
4. Let cook until potatoes are done (about 35–45 minutes).

Nutrition (per serving)
Calories 556
Carbs 36.1 g
Fat 34.8 g
Protein 23.3 g
Sodium 571 mg

Pot Roast

Serves: 6–8
Preparation Time: 10 minutes
Cooking Time: 2 hours 30 minutes

Ingredients
1 (5-pound) round bone pot roast
2 tablespoons olive oil
½ cup barbecue sauce
½ cup red wine or apple cider
1 (14½-ounce) low-sodium beef broth (or 2 cups homemade broth)
2 cups water (or just enough to cover the pot roast)
6 medium carrots, peeled and cut into chunks
6 large potatoes, peeled and quartered
1 large onion, rough chopped
Salt and pepper, to taste

Directions
1. Heat oil in a Dutch oven or heavy bottomed pot on the stovetop or over coals, at medium heat.
2. Sear the meat until browned (about 2 minutes on each side).
3. Remove meat and place on a dish.
4. Add wine or cider to Dutch oven to deglaze. Scrape any bits with a wooden spoon.
5. Return the roast to the pot.
6. Add barbecue sauce, broth, and water.
7. Bring to a gentle simmer and cover with lid.
8. Let cook for 1½ hours.
9. Add the carrots, potatoes, and onions.
10. Replace lid and continue cooking until meat is of desired texture (about 1 hour).
11. Adjust taste with salt and pepper, as needed.
12. Remove from heat and serve.

Nutrition (per serving)
Calories 1101
Carbs 50.2 g
Fat 58.6 g
Protein 86.3 g
Sodium 442 mg

Shepherd's Pie

Serves: 6
Preparation Time: 10 minutes
Cooking Time: 30 minutes

Ingredients
1 pound lean ground beef
1 pound ground sausage
2 cloves garlic, minced
1 medium onion, chopped
2 (12-ounce) packages frozen mixed vegetables
2 (10¾ -ounce) cans cream of mushroom soup
4 cups instant mashed potatoes, prepared according to package instructions
Shredded cheddar cheese, for sprinkling

Directions
1. Heat Dutch oven over medium heat, on stovetop or over hot coals.
2. Cook beef and sausage, stirring frequently, until evenly browned (about 8–10 minutes).
3. Stir in garlic and onion and cook until onions are translucent (about 5 minutes).
4. Press and spread the meat mixture into a single layer over the bottom of the Dutch oven.
5. Pour in cream of mushroom soup and spread to make the second layer.
6. Spread the mixed vegetables on top to make the next layer.
7. Lastly, add the mashed potatoes to make the topmost layer.
8. Cover.

9. Add a ring of hot coals on top of cover.
10. Let cook until oil from lower layer heats up and rises to seep through the mashed potato layer (about 25 minutes).
11. Remove from heat and sprinkle with cheese.

Nutrition (per serving)
Calories 845
Carbs 42.6 g
Fat 45.4 g
Protein 34.7 g
Sodium 2096 mg

Campfire Hash

Serves: 6
Preparation Time: 15 minutes
Cooking Time: 40 minutes

Ingredients
2 tablespoons cooking oil
1 large onion, chopped
2 garlic cloves, minced
4 large potatoes, peeled and cubed
1 pound smoked sausage, cubed
1 (4-ounce) can chopped green chilies
1 (15¼ -ounce) can whole kernel corn, drained

Directions
1. In a cast iron skillet or Dutch oven, heat oil over stovetop or coals.
2. Add onion and garlic, sautéing until onion is translucent (about 3–5 minutes).
3. Stir in potatoes and cook, with occasional stirring, until potatoes are half-cooked (about 15–20 minutes).
4. Stir in sausage and continue cooking until sausages are browned and potatoes are tender (about 10 minutes).
5. Lastly, stir in chilies and corn. Cook until heated through.

Nutrition (per serving)
Calories 535
Carbs 57 g
Fat 26 g
Protein 17 g
Sodium 1097 mg

Camper's Steak Dinner

Serves: 2
Preparation Time: 10 minutes
Cooking Time: 20–30 minutes

Ingredients
1 teaspoon olive oil
1 medium potato, sliced
Salt and pepper, to taste
2 pieces steak (about 1 pound rib eye or flat iron steak)
Steak seasoning, to taste
1 small onion, sliced
1 small carrot, peeled and cut into strips
2 tablespoons butter
2 ice cubes (optional)
Steak sauce of choice (optional)

Directions
1. Stack 2 sheets of aluminum foil together, or use 1 sheet of heavy-duty foil.
2. Drizzle the center of the foil with olive oil.
3. Lay the potato slices in the center, in a single layer. Season with salt and pepper.
4. Season the steak and place on top of potatoes.
5. Add onion and carrot.
6. Season again, as desired.
7. Top with butter.
8. Place ice cubes on top (optional).
9. Fold up sides of foil, leaving room for steaming and expansion because of heat.

10. Seal well to make a packet.
11. Place on preheated grill or on grate over hot coals.
12. Cook to desired doneness (about 20–30 minutes), checking for doneness from time to time. Open carefully to release steam.

Nutrition (per serving)
Calories 580
Carbs 24.9 g
Fat 30.8 g
Protein 49 g
Sodium 514 mg

Fish and Seafood

Moroccan Fish Stew

Serves: 2
Preparation Time: 5 minutes
Cooking Time: 16 minutes

Ingredients

2 tablespoons olive oil
1 small red onion, sliced
2 teaspoons ground cumin
½ teaspoon chili flakes, or to taste
1 medium yellow bell pepper, seeded and sliced into strips
1 (14-ounce) can diced tomatoes, undrained
¾ pound white fish fillets, cut into bite-size pieces
Salt and pepper, to taste

Directions

1. Heat olive oil in skillet or pan over medium heat.
2. Add onion and spices. Sauté until fragrant and onion is translucent (about 3–5 minutes).
3. Add bell pepper and tomatoes.
4. Bring to a gentle simmer and cook until bell pepper is tender (about 3 minutes).
5. Add fish and press down gently into sauce.
6. Cover and keep at a simmer (do not bring to a rolling boil).
7. Fish is done when opaque and easy to flake (about 10 minutes).

Nutrition (per serving)

Calories 334
Carbs 15.1 g
Fat 17.4 g
Protein 32.4 g
Sodium 347 mg

Spicy Shrimp & Tomato Curry

Serves: 2
Preparation Time: 5 minutes
Cooking Time: 10 minutes

Ingredients
1 tablespoon olive oil
1½ teaspoons curry powder, or to taste
1 large red chili, seeded and finely chopped
1½ cups cherry tomatoes
16 large raw prawn cutlets
½ cup coconut cream
Salt and pepper, to taste
Fresh parsley, chopped, for garnish

Directions
1. Heat oil in a pan over medium high heat.
2. Add curry powder and chilies. Sauté until fragrant (about 1 minute).
3. Reduce heat and add tomatoes.
4. Bring to gentle simmer and let simmer for 1 minute.
5. Add prawns and continue cooking until prawns are pink and opaque (about 3–5 minutes).
6. Add coconut cream.
7. Adjust flavor with salt and pepper.
8. Remove from heat and sprinkle with chopped parsley.

Nutrition (per serving)
Calories 142
Carbs 8 g
Fat 8 g
Protein 11 g
Sodium 522 mg

Bacon-Wrapped Trout

Serves: 6
Preparation Time: 20 minutes
Cooking Time: 15 minutes

Ingredients
6 pieces (14–16-ounce) rainbow trout, butterflied and deboned
1 tablespoon Four Seasons Rub (recipe below)
1 bunch fresh parsley
1 bunch fresh thyme
¼ cup fresh sage leaves, thinly sliced
1½ pounds thinly sliced bacon

Four Seasons Rub
1 cup coarse salt
2 tablespoons freshly ground black pepper
2 tablespoons garlic salt
1 teaspoon cayenne pepper

Directions
1. Prepare the Four Seasons Rub. Combine ingredients and pulse in a spice mill until sand-like in texture. Store in an airtight container. Keeps for 1 month.
2. Season trout inside and outside with Four Seasons Rub.
3. Stuff with the herbs and wrap with bacon. This can be done in advance and kept for 6 hours, chilled.
4. Place on preheated grill, flipping over now and then.
5. Fish is done when easily pierced with a paring knife (about 15 minutes).

Nutrition (per serving)
Calories 808
Carbs 2.2 g
Fat 32.7 g
Protein 118.7 g
Sodium 2077mg

Salmon & Potato Foil Packets

Serves: 2
Preparation Time: 15 minutes
Cooking Time: 15 minutes

Ingredients
1 medium potato, sliced as thinly as possible into rounds
4 tablespoons olive oil
Salt and pepper, to taste
2 (6-ounce) salmon filets
1 large orange, halved
1 lemon, halved
Fresh parsley, chopped, for sprinkling

Directions
1. For one serving, stack two sheets of foil together or use one sheet of heavy-duty aluminum foil. Place half of the potato rounds on the center of the foil. Spread out and season with salt and pepper. Drizzle with a tablespoon of olive oil. Place a salmon fillet on top. Season again. Drizzle with the juice of ½ orange and ½ lemon. Drizzle with a second tablespoon of olive oil. Fold over and seal. Repeat to make a second packet with remaining ingredients.
2. Place over a grill preheated to medium-low and cover.
3. Flip over after about 7 minutes.
4. Salmon is done when it is opaque and easily flakes with a fork (about 8–10 minutes longer).
5. Remove from grill and open packets carefully to release steam.
6. Sprinkle with chopped parsley and serve.

Nutrition (per serving)
Calories 388
Carbs 22 g
Fat 24 g
Protein 21 g
Sodium 60 mg

Poor Man's Lobster (Poached Fish)

Serves: 2
Preparation Time: 5 minutes
Cooking Time: 10 minutes

Ingredients
2 cups water
1 tablespoon salt
1 tablespoon minced dried onions
3 tablespoons butter, divided
1 tablespoon dried lemon peel
2 (6-ounce) fish fillets

Directions
1. Combine water, salt, onion, 1 tablespoon butter, and lemon peel in a frying pan.
2. Bring to a simmer.
3. Add fish and cook until opaque and easy to flake with a fork (about 10 minutes).
4. Remove fish and serve with remaining butter.

Nutrition (per serving)
Calories 268
Carbs 1 g
Fat 17.5 g
Protein 22.1 g
Sodium 254 mg

Old Bay Crab Soup

Serves: 1
Preparation Time: 5 minutes
Cooking Time: 25–30 minutes

Ingredients
2 cups water
1½ teaspoons beef bouillon, granules
1 tablespoon dried diced celery
1 tablespoon dried minced onion
1½ teaspoons Old Bay seasoning
2 tablespoons dried diced tomatoes
⅓ cup dried mixed vegetables
⅓ cup dried hash brown potatoes
1 (3½-ounce) package crabmeat

Directions
1. Boil the water in a small pot.
2. Add the other ingredients except for the crabmeat.
3. Bring back to a boil and then reduce to a simmer.
4. When dried vegetables are tender (about 20 minutes), add crabmeat.
5. Simmer for 5–10 minutes.

Nutrition (per serving)
Calories 310
Carbs 47.3 g
Fat 2.6 g
Protein 28.8 g
Sodium 1305 mg

Quick Beer-Battered Fish

Serves: 2
Preparation Time: 20 minutes
Cooking Time: 5–10 minutes

Ingredients
Vegetable oil, for frying
1 pound fish fillets
3 to 4 tablespoons Bisquick

Batter
1 cup Bisquick baking mix
½ cup beer
1 egg
½ teaspoon salt

Directions
1. Wipe fillets dry with paper towels.
2. Coat lightly and evenly with Bisquick.
3. Whisk together ingredients for batter. If too thick, add more beer a little at a time until desired consistency is reached.
4. Dip fillets into batter and gently shake off any excess.
5. Preheat oil in frying pan or cast iron skillet, 1½ inches deep.
6. Fry battered fillets until golden brown (about 2 minutes on each side).
7. Drain.

Nutrition (per serving)
Calories 240
Carbs 23 g
Fat 11 g
Protein 11 g
Sodium 750 mg

Pasta

Mac 'n Cheese

Serves: 4–6
Preparation Time: 5 minutes
Cooking Time: 5 minutes

Ingredients
1 pound elbow macaroni, cooked according to package directions
1 pound sharp cheddar cheese, grated
1 (8-ounce) can diced green chilies, drained
1 (10-ounce) can evaporated milk
¼ cup onion, finely chopped
4 teaspoons ground cumin, or to taste
1 teaspoon kosher or sea salt, or to taste
2 tomatoes, diced

Directions
1. The macaroni may be cooked in advance, drained and tossed in a little oil to prevent sticking. Let cool, then place in a container with lid.
2. Combine the rest of the ingredients, except for the tomatoes, in a large pot.
3. Heat over low heat, with stirring, until cheese is melted.
4. Add cooked pasta and mix.
5. When macaroni is heated through, stir in tomatoes.
6. Serve.

Nutrition (per serving)
Calories 648
Carbs 67.5 g
Fat 29.4 g
Protein 29.3 g
Sodium 952 mg

Southwestern Pasta

Serves: 4
Preparation Time: 10 minutes
Cooking Time: 15 minutes

Ingredients
1 (7 ¼-ounce) package pasta of choice, prepared according to package instructions
1 teaspoon extra virgin olive oil
¼ medium red onion, chopped
½ medium green bell pepper, cut into thin strips
2 tablespoons taco seasoning of choice
1 (8-ounce) can tomatoes and chilies
1 cup frozen corn kernels
2 cups vegetable broth
Salt, to taste
1 (8-ounce) can black beans, drained and rinsed
Shredded cheese, for sprinkling

Directions
1. The pasta may be cooked in advance, drained and tossed in a little oil to prevent sticking. Let cool, then place in a container with lid.
2. Heat the oil in a large pot over medium heat.
3. Add onion, bell pepper, and seasoning. Sauté until fragrant (about 1 minute).
4. Stir in canned tomatoes and corn. Cook a bit until bubbly.
5. Stir in broth and bring to a simmer. Let cook, stirring frequently, until reduced and of desired consistency (about 10–15 minutes).
6. Add cooked pasta and mix. Cook until heated through.
7. Adjust saltiness as needed.
8. Add black beans and remove from heat.
9. Let sit until beans are heated through.
10. Sprinkle with cheese and serve.

Nutrition (per serving)
Calories 320
Carbs 60.1 g
Fat 4.2 g
Protein 11.7 g
Sodium 644 mg

Dutch Oven Lasagna

Serves: 6–8
Preparation Time: 20 minutes
Cooking Time: 40 minutes

Ingredients
1 (9-ounce) package no-boil or oven-ready lasagna noodles
1 pound shredded mozzarella
½ cup grated Parmesan

Meat mixture
½ medium yellow onion, diced
4 cloves garlic, minced
½ pound lean ground beef
1 pound Italian sausage
2 (24-ounce) jars marinara sauce
½ cup water
4 teaspoons sugar
2 teaspoons Italian seasoning
1 teaspoon dried basil
2½ teaspoons salt
½ teaspoon black pepper

Ricotta mixture
16 ounces ricotta cheese
1 egg, beaten
¼ cup finely chopped parsley
1 teaspoon salt

Directions

1. Prepare the meat mixture. Place onion, garlic, beef, and sausage in a skillet over medium high heat and cook, with stirring, until meat is browned. Add the rest of the ingredients for the meat mixture. Simmer for 30 minutes.
2. Prepare the ricotta mixture. Mix the ingredients together in a bowl.
3. Prepare cheese. Combine mozzarella and parmesan in a bowl.
4. Assemble the lasagna. Lightly grease or spray a Dutch oven (preferable 12-inch diameter). Start with a layer of noodles, breaking off corners as needed to fit. Spread with ¼ meat mixture. Spread ¼ of ricotta mixture over meat and then sprinkle with ¼ of the cheese mixture. Repeat layering until ingredients are used up, ending with the cheese mixture. Use broken pasta pieces to fill in gaps.
5. Place Dutch oven over about 9–10 hot briquettes and place about 15–18 briquettes on the lid.
6. Cook for about 40 minutes, rotating the lid every 15 minutes.
7. Remove from heat and remove lid.
8. Let sit for 10 minutes before serving.

Nutrition (per serving)

Calories 689
Carbs 33.7 g
Fat 42.4 g
Protein 40.9 g
Sodium 1706 mg

Backpacker's Spaghetti

Serves: 2–4
Preparation Time: 5 minutes
Cooking Time: 30 minutes

Ingredients

2 cups water
¼ cup dried mushrooms (about ½ cup fresh)
2 tablespoons dried zucchini (about 1 cup fresh)
½ cup dried ground beef (equivalent to 1 pound fresh ground beef)
1 clove fresh garlic
1 cup spaghetti sauce leather (equivalent to one 24-ounce jar)
7 ounces spaghetti noodles, cooked according to package instructions
Parmesan cheese, grated for sprinkling

Directions

1. The pasta may be cooked in advance, drained and tossed in a little oil to prevent sticking. Let cool, then place in a container with lid.
2. Place water in a skillet or saucepan.
3. Add the dried veggies, garlic, beef, and leather.
4. Simmer for 30 minutes or until of correct consistency.
5. To reheat precooked pasta, if needed, submerge in boiling water for about 1 minute and drain.
6. Pour sauce over pasta and sprinkle with Parmesan.

Nutrition (per serving)

Calories 601
Carbs 53.2 g
Fat 28.5 g
Protein 30.3 g
Sodium 830 mg

Vegetarian

Veggie Kebabs

Serves: 10
Preparation Time: 5 minutes plus 30 minutes standing time
Cooking Time: 10 minutes

Ingredients
14 ounces extra firm tofu, cubed
1 red bell pepper, cut into chunks
1 small zucchini, cut into chunks
1 medium onion, quartered and cut into chunks
8 ounces mushrooms, quartered

Marinade
½ cup smooth, unsalted peanut butter
½ cup hot water
2 tablespoons reduced sodium tamari, or soy sauce
2 tablespoons mirin
2 teaspoons sesame oil
¼ teaspoon red pepper flakes
2 cloves garlic, minced

Directions
1. If using bamboo skewers, soak in water for 30 minutes before use.
2. Mix marinade ingredients in a bowl, blending well.
3. Marinate the tofu for 20 minutes.
4. Thread marinated tofu alternately with veggies.
5. Place on preheated grill.
6. Baste with marinade and grill for about 10 minutes.

Nutrition (per serving)
Calories 362
Carbs 22 g
Fat 23 g
Protein 21 g
Sodium 449 mg

Cauliflower & Chickpea Curry

Serves: 6
Preparation Time: 10 minutes
Cooking Time: 30 minutes

Ingredients
2 tablespoons coconut oil
1 large onion, diced
3 cloves garlic, minced
1-inch ginger, peeled and minced
1 tablespoon garam masala or curry powder
2 teaspoons ground coriander
1 teaspoon ground cumin
1 teaspoon ground turmeric
2 (15-ounce) cans chickpeas, drained and rinsed
2 (14½ -ounce) cans diced tomatoes
1 (14-ounce) can coconut milk
1 medium head cauliflower, broken into florets
Salt and pepper, to taste
Chopped cilantro, for sprinkling

Directions
1. Heat coconut oil in Dutch oven over medium heat.
2. Sauté onion, garlic, and ginger until softened (about 5 minutes).
3. Stir in spices until fragrant (about 1 minute).
4. Add chickpeas, coconut milk, and cauliflower.
5. Bring to a boil and then reduce to a simmer.
6. Cover and let simmer for 15 minutes.
7. Remove lid and continue cooking until thickened (about 5 minutes).
8. Remove from heat and season with salt and pepper, as needed.
9. Serve sprinkled with chopped cilantro.

Nutrition (per serving)
Calories 202
Carbs 37.9 g
Fat 3.8 g
Protein 8.7 g
Sodium 406 mg

Corn Casserole

Serves: 12
Preparation Time: 15 minutes
Cooking Time: 60 minutes

Ingredients

2 (8½ -ounce) boxes cornbread or corn muffin mix
2 (15-ounce) cans creamed corn
2 (15-ounce) cans whole kernel corn, drained
2 large eggs
2 cups grated cheese, divided
¼ cup butter, diced

Directions

1. Spray the inside of your Dutch oven with nonstick cooking spray or grease with some cooking oil. Grease the inside of the lid as well.
2. Set aside ½ cup of the cheese.
3. In a bowl, combine all the remaining ingredients.
4. Stir together and pour into Dutch oven.
5. Cover and place on a circle of 7 preheated briquettes.
6. Place 16 briquettes on the lid.
7. Cook for 45 minutes, rotating both the Dutch oven and the lid every 15 minutes.
8. Carefully lift the lid and sprinkle in the remaining cheese.
9. Cook for another 15 minutes.
10. Remove from heat and serve.

Nutrition (per serving)

Calories 342
Carbs 38 g
Fat 15.7 g
Protein 8.8 g
Sodium 769 mg

Mint-Butter Grilled Corn

Serves: 8
Preparation Time: 10 minutes
Cooking Time: 10–15 minutes

Ingredients
8 ears shucked corn

Mint Butter
2 tablespoons butter, softened
1 tablespoon fresh mint, finely chopped
2 teaspoons fresh lemon juice
½ teaspoon fresh cilantro, finely chopped
½ teaspoon coarsely ground black pepper
¼ teaspoon salt

Directions
1. Spray grate with nonstick spray and preheat grill or coals to medium hot.
2. Mix mint-butter ingredients in a bowl and set aside.
3. Place corn on grill.
4. Grill, turning now and them, until kernels are plump and tender (about 10–15 minutes).
5. Transfer to a platter and brush with mint-butter.

Nutrition (per serving)
Calories 149
Carbs 27.4 g
Fat 4.5 g
Protein 4.7 g
Sodium 115 mg

Desserts

Dessert here are not meant to be the healthiest options. If you are looking for healthy, just grill fruits and drizzle them with honey or bake cored apples in a foil packet. But if you want to indulge after a day filled with activities, then you are in for a treat.

Campfire Strawberry Shortcake

Serves: 8
Preparation Time: 15 minutes
Cooking Time: 25 minutes

Ingredients
2⅓ cups Original Bisquick mix
½ cup milk
3 tablespoons sugar
3 tablespoons unsalted butter, at room temperature
2 cups sliced strawberries
Whipped topping

Directions
1. Spray 2 pie tins with nonstick spray or use butter to grease.
2. In a bowl, stir Bisquick mix, milk, sugar, and butter together.
3. Divide the batter into the two greased pie tins.
4. Wrap each in foil, sealing tightly.
5. Place on hot coals.
6. Rotate now and then while cooking until shortcake is golden brown at edges (about 25 minutes).
7. Unwrap and let cool slightly.
8. Top with strawberry slices and whipped topping.

Nutrition (per serving)
Calories 193
Carbs 31.9 g
Fat 5.4 g
Protein 5.1 g
Sodium 504 mg

Grilled Fruit Kebabs

Serves: 6
Preparation Time: 20 minutes
Cooking Time: 15 minutes

Ingredients
½ cup margarine
¼ cup honey
1 teaspoon cinnamon
3 fresh peaches, pitted and quartered
3 fresh plums, pitted and quartered
3 bananas, cut into 4 pieces each
12 strawberries, hulled
Other fruit options: kiwi, grapes, and pineapple; or any other fruit of choice

Directions
1. If using bamboo skewers, soak 12 pieces in water for 30 minutes.
2. Cover grill with aluminum foil and preheat to medium heat.
3. Melt the margarine with the honey and cinnamon in a saucepan. Reduce heat to low and continue cooking until slightly thickened (about 5 minutes). Do not boil.
4. Thread the fruit through skewers.
5. Place on foil-lined grill.
6. Drizzle with margarine-honey mixture.
7. Let grill on one side until fruit becomes tender and sauce is sticky (about 5 minutes).
8. Flip over and drizzle again with sauce.
9. Grill 5 minutes more.
10. Remove from grill and let cool slightly before serving.

Nutrition (per serving)
Calories 268
Carbs 34.8 g
Fat 15.8 g
Protein 1.3 g
Sodium 179 mg

Caramel Apple Crunch

Serves: 1
Preparation Time: 5 minutes
Cooking Time: 10 minutes

Ingredients
1 small apple, cored and chopped
Dash of cinnamon
2 tablespoons caramel syrup
¼ cup granola

Directions
1. Preheat grill to medium heat.
2. Prepare 2 sheets of aluminum foil.
3. Place chopped apple in center of one sheet.
4. Sprinkle with cinnamon, drizzle with caramel syrup, and top with granola.
5. Cover with second sheet of foil.
6. Roll up foil from corners, sealing tightly.
7. Grill until apple is soft (about 10–15 minutes).
8. Open carefully to release hot steam.

Nutrition (per serving)
Calories 308
Carbs 57.9 g
Fat 7.5 g
Protein 5.4 g
Sodium 150 mg

Campfire Fondue

Serves: 8
Preparation Time: 5 minutes
Cooking Time: 5 minutes

Ingredients
⅓ cup milk
3 (1½-ounce) chocolate bars, broken into small pieces
8 marshmallows
Chunks of fruit (like pineapple, strawberry, kiwi, grape, apple, etc.)
4 graham crackers, split into halves (optional)

Directions
1. Fill a small pot with the milk and heat over coals.
2. Heat with continuous stirring until slightly frothy at edges (about 5 minutes). Make sure not to scorch the milk.
3. Remove from heat and add chocolate.
4. Stir until smooth. Place at edge of campfire to keep warm (not hot).
5. Toast marshmallows and fruit, dip into fondue, and sandwich between graham halves (if desired).

Nutrition (per serving)
Calories 138
Carbs 22.4 g
Fat 5.9 g
Protein 1.6 g
Sodium 46 mg

Blueberry & Pineapple Dump Cake

Serves: 8-10
Preparation Time: 20 minutes
Cooking Time: 20–25 minutes

Ingredients
½ (21-ounce) can blueberry pie filling or 1 ½ cup of fresh or frozen blueberries, crushed
1 (8-ounce) can crushed pineapple or 1 cup fresh chopped pineapple with its juices
1 (18½-ounce) boxes yellow cake mix
1 can lemon-lime soda
Optional: Chopped nuts (like walnuts, almonds or pecans)

Directions
1. Heat coals until white.
2. Line Dutch oven with aluminum foil and spray with nonstick cooking spray.
3. Mix the pie filling with the pineapple until well-blended.
4. Scoop the pie filling mixture into the Dutch oven.
5. In a bowl, stir together box cake mix with the soda.
6. Pour batter into Dutch oven, over pie filling.
7. Sprinkle with chopped nuts of choice, if using.
8. Cover.
9. For 10-inch diameter Dutch oven, use 7 coals or briquettes at the bottom and 13 on the lid.
10. Bake until fragrant and toothpick comes out clean when pierced at center of cake, about 20–25 minutes.
11. Remove from Dutch oven. Let cool before serving

Nutrition (per serving)
Calories 376
Carbs 82.9 g
Fat 3.7 g
Protein 3.5 g
Sodium 418 mg

Recipe Index

Also by Louise Davidson

 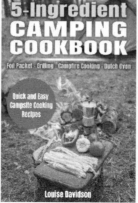 

Appendix

Cooking Conversion Charts

1. Measuring Equivalent Chart

Type	Imperial	Imperial	Metric
Weight	1 dry ounce		28g
	1 pound	16 dry ounces	0.45 kg
Volume	1 teaspoon		5 ml
	1 dessert spoon	2 teaspoons	10 ml
	1 tablespoon	3 teaspoons	15 ml
	1 Australian tablespoon	4 teaspoons	20 ml
	1 fluid ounce	2 tablespoons	30 ml
	1 cup	16 tablespoons	240 ml
	1 cup	8 fluid ounces	240 ml
	1 pint	2 cups	470 ml
	1 quart	2 pints	0.95 l
	1 gallon	4 quarts	3.8 l
Length	1 inch		2.54 cm

* Numbers are rounded to the closest equivalent

2. Oven Temperature Equivalent Chart

Fahrenheit (°F)	Celsius (°C)	Gas Mark
220	100	
225	110	1/4
250	120	1/2
275	140	1
300	150	2
325	160	3
350	180	4
375	190	5
400	200	6
425	220	7
450	230	8
475	250	9
500	260	

* Celsius (°C) = T (°F)-32] * 5/9

** Fahrenheit (°F) = T (°C) * 9/5 + 32

*** Numbers are rounded to the closest equivalent

Recommended Internal Temperature
Cooking Charts for Meats, Poultry and Fish

Beef, Lamb, Roasts, Pork, Veal, Ham

Rare	120 – 130°F (49 – 54°C)
Medium Rare	130 – 135°F (54 – 57°C)
Medium	135 – 145°F (57 – 63°C)
Medium Well	145 – 155°F (64 – 68°C)
Well Done	155°F and greater (68°C)

Pork, ribs

| Fully Cooked | 190 – 205°F (88 – 96°C) |

Poultry

| Fully Cooked | At least 165°F (74°C) |

Fish

| Fully Cooked | At least 130°F (54°C) |

Barbecue Grilling Times

BEEF	Size	Grilling Time	Internal Temperature in °F (Fahrenheit)
Steaks	3/4" thick	3 to 4 min/side 4 to 5 min/side	Medium rare 145 Medium 160
Kabobs	1" cubes	3 to 4 min/side	145 to 160
Hamburger patties	1/2" thick	3 min/side	160
Roast, rolled rump (indirect heat)	4 to 6 lbs.	18 to 22 min/lb.	145 to 160
Sirloin tip (indirect heat)	3 1/2 to 4 lbs.	20 to 25 min/lb.	
Ribs, Back	cut in 1 rib portions	10 min/side	160
Tenderloin	Half, 2 to 3 lbs. Whole, 4 to 6 lbs.	10 to 12 min/side 12 to 15 min/side	Medium rare 145 Medium 160

PORK	Size	Grilling Time	Internal Temperature in °F (Fahrenheit)
Chops, bone in or boneless	3/4" thick	3 to 4 min/side	145
	1 ½" thick	7 to 8 min/side	
Tenderloin	1/2 to 1 1/2 lbs.	15 to 25 min. total	145
Ribs (indirect heat)	2 to 4 lbs.	1 1/2 to 2 hrs.	145
Patties, ground	1/2" thick	4 to 5 min/side	145

HAM	Size	Grilling Time	Internal Temperature in °F (Fahrenheit)
Fully cooked (indirect heat)	Any size	8 to 10 min/lb.	140
Cook before eating (indirect heat)	Whole, 10 to 14 lbs.	10 to 15 min/lb.	160
	Half, 5 to 7 lbs.	12 to 18 min/lb.	
	Portion, 3 to 4 lbs.	30 to 35 min/lb.	

LAMB	Size	Grilling Time	Internal Temperature in °F (Fahrenheit)
Chops, shoulder, loin, or rib	1" thick	5 min/side	145 to 160
Steaks, sirloin, or leg	1" thick	5 min/side	145 to 160
Kabobs	1" cubes	4 min/side	145 to 160
Patties, ground	4 oz., 1/2" thick	3 min/side	160
Leg, butterflied	4 to 7 lbs.	40 to 50 min. total	145 to 160
VEAL	Size	Grilling Time	Internal Temperature in °F (Fahrenheit)
Chops, steaks	1" thick	5 to 7 min/side	145 to 160
Roast, boneless (indirect heat)	2 to 3 lbs.	18 to 20 min/lb.	145 to 160

CHICKEN	Size	Grilling Time	Internal Temperature in °F (Fahrenheit)
Whole (indirect heat), not stuffed	3-4 lbs.	60 to 75 min.	165 to 180 as measured in the thigh
	5-7 lbs.	18 to 25 min/lb.	
	4 - 8 lbs.	15 to 20 min/lb.	
Cornish hens	18-24 oz.	45 to 55 min.	
Breast halves, bone in	6 to 8 oz. each	10 to 15 min/side	165 to 170
boneless	4 oz. each	7 to 8 min./side	
Other parts:			165 to 180
Legs or thighs	4 to 8 oz.	10 to 15 min/side	
Drumsticks	4 oz.	8 to 12 min/side	
Wings,	2 to 3 oz.	8 to 12 min/side	

TURKEY	Size	Grilling Time	Internal Temperature in °F (Fahrenheit)
Whole turkey (indirect heat)	8 to 12 lbs.	2 to 3 hrs.	165 to 180 as measured in the thigh
	12 to 16 lbs.	3 to 4 hrs.	
	16 to 24 lbs.	4 to 5 hrs.	
Breast, bone in	4 to 7 lbs.	1 to 1 3/4 hrs.	165 to 170
boneless	2 3/4 to 3 1/2 lbs.	12 to 15 min/side	
Thighs, drumsticks (indirect heat)	8 to 16 oz.	1 1/2 to 2 hrs.	165 to 180
Direct heat (precook 1 hr.)		8 to 10 min/side	
Boneless turkey roll (indirect heat)	2 to 5 lbs.	1 1/2 to 2 hrs.	165 to 175
	5 to 10 lbs.	2 to 3 1/2 hrs.	

Tips for successful and safe barbecuing:

- To make sure that harmful bacteria, sometime present in uncooked meat and poultry, are destroyed during the cooking process, you must make sure that the internal temperature is high enough for safe consumption. Always use a meat thermometer inserted in the thickest part without touching any bones. Research from the U.S. Department of Agriculture (USDA) states that the color of the meat is not a dependable indicator meat or poultry has reached a temperature high enough to destroy harmful bacteria that may be present.
- Follow this chart for approximate cooking times, Outdoor grills can vary in heat.
- Use barbecue sauce during the last 15 to 30 minutes of grilling to prevent excess browning or burning resulting from the sugars of the sauce.
- USDA recommends cooking pork, beef, veal, lamb chops, ribs and steaks until it reaches a minimum internal temperature of 145ºF and then let rest at least 3 minutes before slicing or consuming.
- Although it is safe to eat poultry with an internal temperature of 165°F, the flavors and the texture are best when the internal temperature reaches 170°F to 180°F

Source: Food Safety and Inspection Service, USDA

Cooking with a Cast Iron Dutch Oven
at the Campsite

When using a cast iron Dutch oven at your campsite, you will usually be applying heat to both the top and the bottom by means of charcoal briquettes. The recipes in this book assume a temperature of approximately 350°F. In order to achieve this, you will use briquettes in numbers that are proportional to the size of your oven. A general rule is to use twice as many briquettes as the diameter of your oven. So for example, if you have a 12-inch oven, you will use 24 pieces of charcoal. A 16-inch oven would require approximately 32. This of course is a very generalized rule that should only serve as a guideline. Always use a thermometer when you are learning to gauge the temperature of your oven, especially if you are using wood rather than coals.

The method of cooking is going to help determine where you place the coals and in what numbers. What this does is help you to distribute the heat at the area where it needs to be most concentrated or distributed. If you are any sautéing, boiling, frying, or open lid cooking, you will place the entire quantity of the coals underneath the oven. For methods of cooking that require both a top and bottom heat source, distribute the coal between the bottom and on top of the lid. Depending on the proportion of heat that you need from each heat source, divide them up with half on top and half on the bottom, or ¾ on the bottom and ¼ on top. Give yourself a little room to practice with adjusting the heat on your Dutch oven before creating more involved meals.

Cooking with your Dutch oven outside is a little different than using it indoors and requires just a few pieces of additional equipment. First of all, you definitely want a good, reliable lid lifting device. Cast iron can be very hot, especially if you have hot coals placed on the lid. To best protect yourself from burns, use a heat protective glove or mitt along with a lid lifting device to remove the lid from the oven. A lid stand is also a good idea. This will provide a heat-proof surface for your lid without setting it on the dirty ground. You may also find a long pair of tongs helpful for moving hot coal briquettes. If you spend a great deal of time cooking in the great outdoors, at some point you may wish to invest in either a tripod or a Dutch oven cooking table. Both of these devices are a little more cumbersome that just the Dutch oven, but they provide a more stable, safer cooking environment to work in.

Foil Packets How To

The best thing about foil packet cooking is that it is extremely easy. You will quickly master all the techniques needed and you will use minimal tools in the process. Here are some of the basic things you need to know when it comes to preparing a foil packet meal for your campsite.

What You Need

Usually, a heat source, cooking spray, aluminum foil and some food are everything you need. Nothing more. Always pick heavy duty aluminum foil as this is better for foil packet cooking. You need to fold it, and heavy duty foil will hold up much better, and it is much handier to use it when you move your packet to the source of heat. This type of foil keeps all crimps and folds you made and you will be sure that all the steam and juices are held in the foil.

Heat Sources

Any heat source will serve well for foil packet cooking, so you can use a grill, fire pit or propane source of heat. What you need to make sure of is not to place the foil packets you make directly on the flame. When using a fire pit or a grill, you want to prepare it by setting fire to some coals or wood. Let the fire burn down until the coals or wood are really hot but without open flame. Arrange the packets to cook so they are a few inches away from the heat source, and turn them occasionally for even cooking.

Cooking Sprays and Fats

Always make sure to spray the foil with cooking spray. You don't want your food to stick to the foil or get charred. The only situation when you can skip this step is if the food you are preparing already has enough oil to provide an adequate protective coating. Alternatives to cooking spray include melted butter or cooking oil; a light brushing of either of these is equally effective.

Feel Free to Experiment, But Keep Your Ingredients in Mind

When you start discovering the endless possibilities foil packet cooking offers, you will want to make your own packets. You should definitely try this, so feel free to experiment! There is one thing to keep in mind here, and that is the size and type of the ingredients you want to mix. For example, thin pieces of meat can only be combined with thinly sliced vegetables. You see, hard vegetables need longer cooking times, so if you mix them with thinly sliced meat, you will end up either undercooking the vegetables or overcooking the meat, simply because you put them both in one foil packet.

Always think of the cooking process when you choose your ingredients. Other good advice is to have at least one ingredient with a certain level of moisture, especially if the recipe you are creating is rather dry. In foil packet cooking, it's a tricky thing to add the ingredients once the cooking process has begun. This is why you need to be sure that you have made the right combination before you start. Tomatoes, marinades, and butter are examples of ingredients with moisture you can use.

Assembly

When you prepare your packets, keep in mind the variable cooking times for the ingredients you are using. The ingredients that need to be cooked the longest should be placed at the bottom of the foil, so they will have the most exposure to the source of heat.

Let's take an example. If you're combining meat with vegetables, a good choice is to put the meat to the bottom of the foil and then top it with vegetables, because meat demands longer cooking time. Another thing to note is the blending and texture of the ingredients you use. When you have an ingredient that will melt, like cheese, then put it nearest to the ingredient you want to mix it with so you can get the best flavor possible.

Styles of packets

You can choose between two different foil packet styles, depending on the ingredients you use when you prepare the packet.

The Flat Packet

This type of packet is tighter and keeps the ingredients closer together. It produces less steam and it is perfect for meals you want charred or seared. Note that less steam means less moisture in flat packets, which is why you need to be sure that you have enough ingredients with moisture and not only dry ingredients. Only when you are sure of this should you begin the cooking process. Trust me, just adding some butter is more than enough to make a difference between a juicy steak and the one that is dry and tough.

What you need to do to make a flat packet is take a sheet of aluminum foil and spray it on the inside. Lay the foil on a flat surface and put your ingredients in the middle, layering in accordance with the type and size of the ingredients. Do not spread out your ingredients too much. They should be compact and you will need some free surface around the outside foil edges.

Take two longer foil edges and fold them up to meet in the center. Then make large downward folds toward your ingredients. Bring the packet's short ends in toward the middle and crimp the foil to form a secure, tight packet. When putting the packet on your heat source, make sure to place the folded side up.

The Tent Packet

When you need more steaming and heat circulation, you should opt to use tent packets. Any packet that contains grains or produce will be better cooked in a tent packet. Actually, the only difference between the two styles is that there is more space between the top of the packet and the food, but this allows the food to steam.

Tent packets are made so the top doesn't touch your food. Leave about one to three inches of space above your ingredients. Use a large piece of heavy duty aluminum foil (remember to spray it), and make sure it is big enough to fit all your ingredients. Allow more foil around the sides because you want enough space for airflow at the top. You also need enough left to make a secure crimp at the top.

Put your ingredients in the middle of the foil. Fold up the long ends of the foils over the food, meeting in the center a couple of inches above the ingredients. Use small folds to crease the foil until you are sure that its top is about three inches distant from the food. Crimp the top tightly. Bring in the sides just close enough to produce a strong seal on each side. When putting the packet over a heat source, place the folded side up.

Made in the USA
Middletown, DE
29 November 2022

16468563R00055